W9-CTV-762

The Power of a
PRAYING®
WIFE
DEVOTIONAL
JOURNAL

Reflections from
STORMIE OMARTIAN

HARVEST HOUSE PUBLISHERS
EUGENE, OREGON

The Power of a Praying® Wife Devotional Journal

Text copyright © 2002 by Stormie Omartian

Published by Harvest House Publishers
Eugene, Oregon 97402
www.harvesthousepublishers.com

ISBN 978-0-7369-5322-1

Design and production by Franke Design & Illustration
Excelsior, MN 55331

All Scripture quotations are from the New King James Version. Copyright © 1982 by
Thomas Nelson, Inc. Used by permission. All rights reserved.

All rights reserved. No part of this publication may be reproduced, stored in a retrieval system, or
transmitted in any form or by any means—electronic, mechanical, digital, photocopy, recording, or any
other—except for brief quotations in printed reviews, without the prior permission of the publisher.

Printed in China

13 14 15 16 17 18 19 / RDS / 10 9 8 7 6 5 4 3 2 *

Welcome to a life of prayer...

*K*eeping a prayer journal as you pray for your husband is probably one of the most important things you can do to benefit your marriage. Writing out your thoughts, feelings, desires, and conversations with God is not only healing and liberating, but it also gives you a fresh perspective on how to pray. I have found that as I put down my own thoughts and concerns on paper, I gain new insight into the very thing I am writing about. It gives me increased clarity. I find a deeper level of understanding about my husband, myself, our marriage, and the details of our lives together. You, too, can experience all that. But don't think of this as merely writing down a list of concerns. Think of it as sharing your heart with the Lord and expressing your deepest feelings and needs to Him. Think of it as presenting your thoughts, questions, and prayer requests to God and allowing Him to lift any burden from you and clear your mind of all worry.

I pray that each of the short prayers and scriptures I have included here will inspire and motivate you to write in greater detail on those particular subjects, and to include any other areas of prayer need that they may bring to your mind. As you write, be sure to include anything God reveals to you or impresses upon your heart. He will speak to your soul through His Word or as you are in prayer. His words to you are as important as yours are to Him. Preserve them on these pages as precious gems. May God bless you and your marriage as you travel on this prayer journey with the Lord.

—Stormie Omartian

Continue earnestly in prayer, being vigilant
in it with thanksgiving.

COLOSSIANS 4:2

Lord, give me a fresh perspective, a positive
outlook, and a renewed relationship with the
man You've given me. Only You are perfect,
and I look to You to perfect us. Help me see
him with new eyes, new appreciation,
new love, new compassion, and new
acceptance. Teach me how to pray for my
husband and make my prayers a true
language of love. Make me a new person.
Give my husband a new wife, Lord,
and let it be me.

Continue earnestly in prayer, being vigilant in it with thanksgiving.

COLOSSIANS 4:2

...teach me how to pray

But the fruit of the Spirit is love, joy, peace, longsuffering, kindness, goodness, faithfulness, gentleness, self-control.

GALATIANS 5:22-23

*L*ord, make me my husband's helpmate, companion, champion, friend, and support. Help me to create a peaceful, restful, safe place for him to come home to. Teach me how to take care of myself and stay attractive to him. Grow me into a creative and confident woman who is rich in mind, soul, and spirit. Make me the kind of woman he can be proud to say is his wife.

But the fruit of the Spirit is love, joy, peace, longsuffering, kindness, goodness, faithfulness, gentleness, self-control.

GALATIANS 5:22-23

...helpmate, companion, champion, friend

When you eat the labor of your hands, you shall be happy, and it shall be well with you.

Psalm 128:2

*L*ord, I pray that my husband's work will be established, secure, successful, satisfying, and financially rewarding. I pray that You will be Lord over his work, and may he bring You into every aspect of it. Give him enough confidence in the gifts You've placed in him to be able to seek, find, and do good work. Open up doors of opportunity for him that no man can close. Develop his skills so that they grow more valuable with each passing year. Show me what I can do to encourage him.

When you eat the labor of your hands, you shall be happy, and it shall be well with you.

PSALM 128:2

...be Lord over his work

As for every man to whom God has given riches and wealth, and given him power to eat of it, to receive his heritage and rejoice in his labor—this is the gift of God.

ECCLESIASTES 5:19

Lord, I pray that (husband's name) will find it easy to give to You and to others as You have instructed in Your Word. Give him wisdom to handle money wisely. Help him make good decisions as to how he spends. Show him how to plan for the future. I pray that he will find the perfect balance between spending needlessly and being miserly. May he always be paid well for the work he does, and may his money not be stolen, lost, devoured, destroyed, or wasted.

As for every man to whom God has given riches and wealth, and given him power to eat of it, to receive his heritage and rejoice in his labor—this is the gift of God.

ECCLESIASTES 5:19

...help him handle money wisely

I have been young, and now am old; yet I have not seen the righteous forsaken, nor his descendants begging bread.

PSALM 37:25

*L*ord, help both of us to remember that all we have belongs to You and to be grateful for it. May we be good stewards of all that You give us, and walk in total agreement as to how it is to be dispersed. I pray that we will learn to live free of burdensome debt. Where we have not been wise, bring restoration and give us guidance. Show me how I can help increase our finances and not decrease them unwisely.

I have been young, and now am old; yet I have not seen the righteous forsaken, nor his descendants begging bread.

PSALM 37:25

...all we have belongs to You

Drink water from your own cistern, and running water from your own well. Should your fountains be dispersed abroad, streams of water in the streets? Let them be only your own, and not for strangers with you. Let your fountain be blessed, and rejoice with the wife of your youth.

PROVERBS 5:15-18

Lord, I realize that an important part of my ministry to my husband is sexual. Help me to never use sex as a weapon or a means of manipulation by giving and withholding it for selfish reasons. I commit this area of our lives to You, Lord. May it be continually new and alive. Make it all that You created it to be. I pray that we will desire each other and no one else. Show me how to make myself attractive and desirable to my husband and be the kind of partner he needs. I pray that neither of us will ever be tempted to think about seeking fulfillment elsewhere.

Drink water from your own cistern, and running water from your own well. Should your fountains be dispersed abroad, streams of water in the streets? Let them be only your own, and not for strangers with you. Let your fountain be blessed, and rejoice with the wife of your youth.

PROVERBS 5:15-18

...be the kind of partner he needs

If anyone is in Christ, he is a new creation; old things have passed away; behold, all things have become new.

2 Corinthians 5:17

*L*ord, deliver us from the bondage of past mistakes. Remove from our midst the effects of any sexual experience—in thought or deed—that happened outside of our relationship. Take away anyone or anything from our lives that would inspire temptation to infidelity. Help us to "abstain from sexual immorality" so that each of us will know "how to possess his own vessel in sanctification and honor" (1 Thessalonians 4:4). I pray that we will make time for one another, communicate our true feelings openly, and remain sensitive to what each other needs.

If anyone is in Christ, he is a new creation; old things have passed away; behold, all things have become new.

2 CORINTHIANS 5:17

...sanctification and honor

If there is any consolation in Christ, if any comfort of love, if any fellowship of the Spirit, if any affection and mercy, fulfill my joy by being like-minded, having the same love, being of one accord, of one mind.

PHILIPPIANS 2:1-2

Lord, help my husband and me to demonstrate how much we care for and value each other. Remind us throughout each day to affectionately touch one another in some way. Help us to not be cold, undemonstrative, uninterested, or remote. Enable us to be warm, tender, compassionate, loving, and adoring. Break through any hardheadedness on our part that refuses to change and grow. If one of us is less affectionate to the other's detriment, bring us into balance.

If there is any consolation in Christ, if any comfort of love, if any fellowship of the Spirit, if any affection and mercy, fulfill my joy by being like-minded, having the same love, being of one accord, of one mind.

PHILIPPIANS 2:1-2

...warm, tender, compassionate, loving

His left hand is under my head, and his
right hand embraces me.

SONG OF SOLOMON 2:6

*L*ord, may we not so take each other for granted
that we don't make the effort to reach out and
touch each other with affection. Help us not to
weaken our marriage through neglect of this vital
means of communication. I pray that we always
"greet one another with a kiss of love" (1 Peter 5:14).
I know that only the transforming power of the
Holy Spirit can make changes that last.
I trust You to transform us and make us the
husband and wife You called us to be.

His left hand is under my head, and his right hand embraces me.

SONG OF SOLOMON 2:6

...let us touch each other with affection

Blessed is the man who endures temptation; for when he has been approved, he will receive the crown of life which the Lord has promised to those who love Him.

JAMES 1:12

*L*ord, I pray that (husband's name) will not be broken down by the power of evil, but raised up by the power of God. Establish a wall of protection around him. Fill him with Your Spirit and flush out all that is not of You. Help him to take charge over his own spirit and have self-control to resist anything and anyone who becomes a lure. I pray that You would strengthen my husband to resist any temptation that comes his way.

Blessed is the man who endures temptation; for when he has been approved, he will receive the crown of life which the Lord has promised to those who love Him.

JAMES 1:12

...fill him with Your Spirit

Examine me, O Lord, and prove me; try my mind and my heart. For Your lovingkindness is before my eyes, and I have walked in Your truth.

Psalm 26:2-3

Lord, shield my husband's mind from the lies of the enemy. Help him to clearly discern between Your voice and any other, and show him how to take every thought captive as You have instructed us to do. May he thirst for Your Word and hunger for Your truth so that he can recognize wrong thinking. Remind him again today that he has the mind of Christ.

Examine me, O LORD, and prove me; try my mind and my heart. For Your lovingkindness is before my eyes, and I have walked in Your truth.

PSALM 26:2-3

...he has the mind of Christ

*You will keep him in perfect peace, whose mind is
stayed on You, because he trusts in You.*

ISAIAH 26:3

*L*ord, help (husband's name) to be anxious for
nothing, but in everything by prayer and
supplication, with thanksgiving, let his requests
be made known to You; and may Your peace,
which surpasses all understanding, guard his
heart and mind through Christ Jesus
(Philippians 4:6-7). And whatever things are
true, noble, just, pure, lovely, of good report,
having virtue, or anything praiseworthy, let him
think on these things (Philippians 4:8).

You will keep him in perfect peace, whose mind is stayed on You, because he trusts in You.

ISAIAH 26:3

...guard his heart and mind

The Lord is my light and my salvation;
whom shall I fear? The Lord is the strength
of my life; of whom shall I be afraid?

Psalm 27:1

Lord, I pray You will perfect (husband's name)
in Your love so that fear finds no place in him.
I know You have not given him a spirit of fear.
You've given him power, love, and a sound mind
(2 Timothy 1:7). I pray in the name of Jesus that
fear will not rule over (husband's name). Instead,
may Your Word penetrate every fiber of his
being, convincing him that Your love for him is
far greater than anything he faces and
nothing can separate him from it.

The Lord is my light and my salvation; whom shall I fear? The Lord is the strength of my life; of whom shall I be afraid?

PSALM 27:1

...power, love, and a sound mind

Behold, the eye of the Lord is on those who fear Him, on those who hope in His mercy.

PSALM 33:18

*L*ord, deliver (husband's name) this day from fear that destroys and replace it with godly fear (Jeremiah 32:40). Teach him Your way, O Lord. Help him to walk in Your truth. Unite his heart to fear Your name (Psalm 86:11). May he have no fear of men, but rise up and boldly say, "The Lord is my helper; I will not fear. What can man do to me?" (Hebrews 13:6) and, "How great is Your goodness, which You have laid up for those who fear You, which You have prepared for those who trust in You" (Psalm 31:19).

Behold, the eye of the LORD is on those who fear Him, on those who hope in His mercy.

PSALM 33:18

...how great is Your goodness

As God has distributed to each one, as the Lord
has called each one, so let him walk.

1 Corinthians 7:17

*L*ord, when You call us, You also enable us.
Enable my husband to walk worthy of his calling
and become the man of God You made him to be.
Continue to remind him of what You've called
him to, and don't let him get sidetracked with
things that are unessential to Your plan for his
life. Lift his eyes above the circumstances of
the moment so he can see the purpose for
which You created him.

As God has distributed to each one, as the Lord has called each one, so let him walk.

1 CORINTHIANS 7:17

... You call us for Your purposes

May He grant you according to your heart's desire,
and fulfill all your purpose.

PSALM 20:4

Lord, help (husband's name) to realize who he
is in Christ and give him certainty that he was
created for a high purpose. May the eyes of
his understanding be enlightened so that he
will know what is the hope of Your calling
(Ephesians 1:18). I pray that the desires of his
heart will not be in conflict with the desires
of Yours. May he seek You for direction,
and hear when You speak to his soul.

May He grant you according to your heart's desire, and fulfill all your purpose.

PSALM 20:4

...created for a high purpose

But as for me, I would seek God, and to God
I would commit my cause.

JOB 5:8

Lord, give (husband's name) daily discernment
to make decisions based on Your revelation. Help
him to make godly choices and keep him from
doing anything foolish. Take foolishness out of
his heart and enable him to quickly recognize
error and avoid it. Open his eyes to clearly see
the consequences of any anticipated behavior.
May he reverence You and Your ways and
seek to know Your truth.

But as for me, I would seek God, and to God I would commit my cause.

JOB 5:8

...make godly choices

If any of you lacks wisdom, let him ask of God,
who gives to all liberally and without reproach,
and it will be given to him.

James 1:5-6

*L*ord, please instruct my husband even as he is
sleeping (Psalm 16:7), and in the morning,
I pray he will do what's right rather than follow
the leading of his own flesh. I know the wisdom
of this world is foolishness with You, Lord
(1 Corinthians 3:19). May he not buy into it,
but keep his eyes on You and have ears
to hear Your voice.

*If any of you lacks wisdom, let him ask of God, who gives to all liberally
and without reproach, and it will be given to him.*

JAMES 1:5-6

...give him ears to hear Your voice

Bless the LORD, O my soul, and forget not all
His benefits: who forgives all your iniquities,
who heals all your diseases.

PSALM 103:2-3

*L*ord, when my husband is ill, I pray You will
sustain him and heal him. Fill him with Your joy
to give him strength. Specifically, I pray for
(mention any area of concern). Give him faith to
say, "'O LORD my God, I cried out to You, and
You healed me' (Psalm 30:2). Thank You,
Lord, that You are my healer." I pray that my
husband will live a long and healthy life.

Bless the LORD, O my soul, and forget not all His benefits: who forgives all your iniquities, who heals all your diseases.

PSALM 103:2-3

...fill him with Your joy

Beloved, I pray that you may prosper in all things and be in health, just as your soul prospers.

3 John 1:2

𝓛ord, I pray that (husband's name) will have the desire to take care of his body, to eat the kind of food that brings health, to get regular exercise, and avoid anything that would be harmful to him. Help him to understand that his body is Your temple, and he should care for it as such (1 Corinthians 3:16). I pray that he will present it as a living sacrifice, holy and acceptable to You (Romans 12:1).

Beloved, I pray that you may prosper in all things and be in health, just as your soul prospers.

3 JOHN 1:2

...holy and acceptable to You

The Lord *is my rock and my fortress and my deliverer;*
my God, my strength, in whom I will trust; my shield
and the horn of my salvation, my stronghold. I will call
upon the Lord, *who is worthy to be praised;*
so shall I be saved from my enemies.

Psalm 18:2-3

Lord, watch over my husband, and keep him safe,
especially in cars and planes. Hide him from
violence and the plans of evil people. Wherever
he walks, secure his steps. Keep him on Your path
so that his feet don't slip (Psalm 17:5). If his foot
does slip, hold him up by Your mercy (Psalm 94:18).
Give him the wisdom and discretion that will
help him walk safely and not fall into danger
(Proverbs 3:21-23).

The LORD is my rock and my fortress and my deliverer; my God, my strength, in whom I will trust; my shield and the horn of my salvation, my stronghold. I will call upon the LORD, who is worthy to be praised; so shall I be saved from my enemies.

PSALM 18:2-3

...hold him up by Your mercy

In the time of trouble He shall hide me in His pavilion;
in the secret place of His tabernacle He shall hide me;
He shall set me high upon a rock.

PSALM 27:5

*L*ord, I pray today that You would be my husband's fortress, strength, shield, and stronghold (Psalm 18:2-3). Make him to dwell in the shadow of Your wings (Psalm 91:1-2). Be his rock, salvation, and defense, so that he will not be moved or shaken (Psalm 62:6). I pray that even though bad things may be happening all around him, they will not come near him (Psalm 91:7).

In the time of trouble He shall hide me in His pavilion; in the secret place of His tabernacle He shall hide me; He shall set me high upon a rock.

PSALM 27:5

...the shadow of Your wings

Cast your burden on the LORD, and He shall sustain you; He shall never permit the righteous to be moved.

PSALM 55:22

Lord, I know You work great things in the midst of trials. Help me support (husband's name) with prayer and encouragement so that he will get through every battle as a winner. You are our refuge and strength, a very present help in trouble (Psalm 46:1). Build up my husband so that no matter what happens he will be able to stand strong through it.

Cast your burden on the LORD, and He shall sustain you; He shall never permit the righteous to be moved.

PSALM 55:22

...our refuge and strength

Through the LORD's mercies we are not consumed, because His compassions fail not. They are new every morning; great is Your faithfulness.

LAMENTATIONS 3:22-23

*L*ord, You have invited us to "come boldly to the throne of grace, that we may obtain mercy and find grace to help in time of need" (Hebrews 4:16). I come before Your throne and ask for grace for my husband. Strengthen his heart for this battle and give him patience to wait on You (Psalm 27:1-4). Help him to be always "rejoicing in hope, patient in tribulation, continuing steadfastly in prayer" (Romans 12:12).

Through the LORD's mercies we are not consumed, because His compassions fail not. They are new every morning; great is Your faithfulness.

LAMENTATIONS 3:22-23

...obtain mercy and find grace

Let integrity and uprightness preserve me,
for I wait for You.

PSALM 25:21

$\mathcal{L}$ord, I pray You would help (husband's name) to be a man of great integrity. Guide him by Your Spirit of truth at all times (John 16:13). Be with him to bear witness to the truth so that in times of pressure he will act on it with confidence. Bind mercy and truth around his neck and write them on the tablet of his heart so he will find favor and high esteem in the sight of God and man (Proverbs 3:3-4).

Let integrity and uprightness preserve me, for I wait for You.

PSALM 25:21

...favor and high esteem

Vindicate me, O Lord, for I have walked in my integrity. I have also trusted in the Lord; I shall not slip.

PSALM 26:1

Lord, give my husband the strength to say "yes" when he should say "yes," and courage to say "no" when he should say "no." Enable him to stand for what he knows is right and not waver under pressure from the world. Give him a teachable spirit that is willing to listen to the voice of wisdom and grow in Your ways.

Vindicate me, O Lord, for I have walked in my integrity. I have also trusted in the Lord; I shall not slip.

PSALM 26:1

...grow in Your ways

By humility and the fear of the LORD
are riches and honor and life.

PROVERBS 22:4

*L*ord, I pray over my husband's reputation.
I ask that (husband's name) will bear good fruit
out of the goodness that is within him, and that
he will be known by the good that he does.
May the fruits of honesty, trustworthiness,
and humility sweeten all his dealings so that
his reputation will never be spoiled.

By humility and the fear of the LORD are riches and honor and life.

PROVERBS 22:4

...be known by the good that he does

Who shall bring a charge against God's elect? It is God who justifies. Who is he who condemns? It is Christ who died, and furthermore is also risen, who is even at the right hand of God, who also makes intercession for us.

Lord, may (husband's name) trust in You and not be afraid of what man can do to him (Psalm 56:11). For You have said whoever believes in You will not be put to shame (Romans 10:11). Lead him, guide him, and be his mighty fortress and hiding place. May his light so shine before men that they see his good works and glorify You, Lord (Matthew 5:16).

Who shall bring a charge against God's elect? It is God who justifies. Who is he who condemns? It is Christ who died, and furthermore is also risen, who is even at the right hand of God, who also makes intercession for us.

ROMANS 8:33-34

...may his light shine

A faithful man will abound with blessings.

PROVERBS 28:20

*L*ord, speak to (husband's name) about making
Your Word, prayer, and praise a priority.
Enable him to place our children and me in
greater prominence in his heart than career,
friends, and activities. I pray he will seek
You first and submit his all to You, for when
he does I know the other pieces of his life
will fit together perfectly.

A faithful man will abound with blessings.

PROVERBS 28:20

...seek You first

Mark the blameless man, and observe the upright;
for the future of that man is peace.

Psalm 37:37

*L*ord, may (husband's name) live with leading
from the Holy Spirit and not walk in doubt and
fear of what may happen in the days that lie
ahead. Help him to mature and grow in You daily,
submitting to You all his dreams and desires,
knowing that "the things which are impossible
with men are possible with God" (Luke 18:27).
Give him God-ordained goals, and show him
how to conduct himself in a way that
always invests in his future.

Mark the blameless man, and observe the upright; for the future of that man is peace.

PSALM 37:37

...all his dreams and desires

There is hope in your future, says the LORD.

JEREMIAH 31:17

Lord, I pray that You would plant my husband firmly in Your house and keep him fresh and flourishing and bearing fruit into old age (Psalm 92:13-14). And when it comes time for him to leave this earth and go to be with You, may he have such a strong vision for his eternal future that it makes his transition smooth, painless, and accompanied by peace and joy. Until that day, I pray he will find the vision for his future in You.

There is hope in your future, says the Lord.

JEREMIAH 31:17

....

....

....

....

....

....

....

....

....

....

....

....

....

....

....

....

...his eternal future

Then our mouth was filled with laughter,
and our tongue with singing...
The LORD has done great things for us,
and we are glad.

PSALM 126:2-3